Dedicated to my nine grandchildren: Henry, Adrienne, Shane, Carson, Lucien, Eli, Colette, Cecilia and Lumina, as well as to the McKeldin family and Baltimore's mounted police and their horses, especially Charlie, who was Sergeant Bill's first mount.

—P.E.D.

Dedicated to my mother for her loving support and to my teacher, Shadra Strickland, for her endless guidance and encouragement.

—M.G.C

The material on Sergeant Bill, a real person, was gleaned mainly from articles in the *Baltimore Sun*. I am grateful to their authors Frank Henry (1946), Peter Q. Allison (1951), Ralph Reppert and Hans Marx (1962), Jacques Kelly (1996) and Frederick N. Rasmussen (2004), as well as Gilbert Sandler, whose essay "Wrong McKeldin Honored?" in his book *Baltimore Glimpses Revisited*, first suggested that Sergeant Bill also be honored in McKeldin Square. The part of the story involving President Franklin Delano Roosevelt and his dog Fala is fictional.

To the Library for many girls to enjoy —

Sergeant Bill and His Horse Bob

Peter E. Dans
5/3/16

Peter E. Dans

Illustrated by
Mary Grace
Corpus

Camino Books, Inc.
Philadelphia

Harborplace is one of the coolest places to visit in Baltimore. There you can see blacktip sharks swimming at the National Aquarium and you can board the *USS Constellation*, built in 1854 to replace the original 1797 frigate of the same name.

But if you could travel back 75 years, you wouldn't find Harborplace. Instead you would see a very busy waterfront crowded with longshoremen loading and unloading ships as well as passengers headed for the ferries to the Eastern Shore of Maryland and Virginia.

It was the site of the nation's busiest intersection at Pratt and Light Streets on the road from New York City to Florida. In those days before Interstate 95, the Baltimore Beltway and the Harbor Tunnel, you would see cars, trucks and horse-drawn wagons, jockeying with each other as well as fearless pedestrians trying to cross the street.

In those early days, no traffic light ordered the chaos, but from 1937 to 1955, a mounted policeman named Sergeant Bill McKeldin and his faithful horse Bob directed traffic. Bill stood on a six-foot-high platform to which was attached a pole with the words STOP and GO.

Officer McKeldin signals a motorist to stop, saying, "Can't you see the sign?"

Later the city built a kiosk where Sergeant Bill kept an eagle eye and would wave and shout to keep traffic flowing. Bill always gave credit to his horse Bob, who had learned to position himself in the direction of the traffic flow.

Sometimes Sergeant Bill had to go down and untangle the traffic; Sergeant Bill tells motorists to "Move it."

Sometimes he answered questions from lost drivers.

Time to change directions as Bill and
Bob orchestrate the flow almost like a ballet.

A truck driver from St. Louis called Sergeant Bill the "Whistler of Pratt and Light Street" because of the way he used to whistle through his teeth as he signaled the drivers of cars and trucks. He didn't think the police whistle was loud enough, and in fact it was said that his whistling could be heard three blocks away.

Whenever he would whistle, the truck drivers and children used
to whistle and wave back at him.

Some would call him by his nickname "Podge," but most called out the name of famous horseback riders like the Lone Ranger, Hopalong Cassidy, Paul Revere, and Renfrew of the Royal Mounted. When anyone asked him what he did for a living, he said he was in the Cavalry.

Bill and Bob were great friends, and Bob used to nibble Bill's ear when he visited the stable, but he never hurt him.

When Bill wasn't wearing his policeman's uniform, Bob would turn away even when Bill offered him his favorite chestnuts.

Sergeant Bill's brother was the Mayor of Baltimore and later Governor of Maryland, so Bill never considered himself very important. Even though everyone loved him, he thought of himself as the family "eight ball."

That all changed the day the President of the United States, Franklin Delano Roosevelt, stopped to talk to Bill on his way from Washington to his family home in Hyde Park, New York.

While they were talking, the president's beloved dog, Fala, spotted a cat and jumped out of the car.

Fala chased the cat down the harbor and around the crates. Bob and Bill stopped the traffic and started after them, but they were no match for Fala and the cat, who were easily able to get around the longshoremen and all the crates being loaded onto the Grace Line ship *Santa Rosa*.

Bound for South America, the ship was just raising its gangplank and anchor with a tugboat positioned to direct it out of the harbor.

There were no cell phones in those days, and it was up to Bill and Bob to get the attention of the captain. So they raced down Light Street onto the cobblestones of Federal Hill, narrowly missing an Arabber selling his fruits and vegetables.

When they reached Fort McHenry, they stopped and Bill whistled and waved to the tugboat captain to head the *Santa Rosa* back to the dock, where an anxious president waited.

When Bill and Bob returned, President Roosevelt thanked them for rescuing Fala. Then he placed a garland of black-eyed Susans around Bob's neck. These are the same flowers that are draped on the horses that win the famous race at nearby Pimlico racetrack in Baltimore.

If you visit downtown Baltimore, you will see a much different, but still busy, intersection at Pratt and Light Streets. Close by is McKeldin Square, named after Sergeant Bill's brother, where an ice skating rink operates during the winter. I like to think that it also honors Sergeant Bill and Bob, who spent so many years bringing smiles to countless motorists and whose ghosts may be seen in your mind's eye, if you look hard enough.